THE STORY OF JERUSALEM

JAMES PARKES

The Story of

JERUSALEM

LONDON
THE CRESSET PRESS
1949

First published in 1949 by
The Cresset Press Ltd., 11 Fitzroy Square, London, W.1

Printed in Great Britain by
The Narod Press, 129-131 Cavell Street, London, E.1

CONTENTS

MAPS

NOTE

I would like to express my gratitude to Bertha Urdang of Jerusalem for a great deal of information about the modern city and the siege, and to Leslie R. Thurston for the maps.

JAMES PARKES

INTRODUCTION

THE MANY proposals which are being put forward for the future
of Jerusalem cannot be understood except on a basis of its long
history, its geographical position, its rapid development in the
last century, and the siege through which its Jewish population
have just passed. The purpose of this pamphlet is to give the
relevant facts which must form the data for the discussion of any
durable solution. The facts are complicated and sometimes con-
tradictory, and many have a high emotional content to the
adherents of three religions scattered through the world.

. Emotional factors cannot be ignored by politicians, but even
these have to be weighed one against another; for emotions can
be stimulated by propaganda as well as produced by actual circumstances. It is not necessarily statesmanship to give equal
value to all emotional claims, or to ignore the evidence of the
depth and sincerity of an emotion which is provided by the
extent to which it has been translated into the buildings,
institutions, human lives and sacrifices which make up the
Jerusalem of to-day.

In its ancient Holy Places, in its modern towers and spires,
in the number of its churches and convents, schools and hospitals,
centres of learning and piety, Jerusalem testifies to the devotion
of Christians in all parts of the world to the Holy City. It is
perhaps unfair to expect a similar showing from Muslims, for
Jerusalem is the third, not the first, of their holy cities. But the
spacious beauty of the Haram ash-Sharif, with the Dome of the
Rock and the mosque of Aqsa, still dominates the old town, and
enjoys the veneration of the Muslim world; and Muslims of the
whole region join once a year in Jerusalem for the pilgrimage of
Nebi Musa to the ' Tomb of Moses ' on the Jericho road.

But the city of Jerusalem to-day, as a city in which men live
and work and express their ideals in practical living, is pre-
eminently a Jewish city—a city of Jewish homes, streets and
shops, of Jewish factories and professions, of Jewish institutions
of religion, learning and philanthropy (a philanthropy which
has endowed research, hospitals and clinics for the use of all the
inhabitants impartially). Ever since Jerusalem began to grow

from a medieval walled city, Jews have formed two-thirds of its population.

But Jerusalem has become still more a Jewish city because of the experiences of a hundred thousand Jewish men, women, and children during the bitter siege of 1948. Nor can they forget either that they were almost reduced to starvation in the actual presence of the British Administration which, until May 15, 1948, claimed the sole responsibility for the maintenance of law and order in the city, or that they owed their deliverance only to their own valour and endurance.

These are factors as real as the ancient religious emotions which Jews share with Christians and Muslims; and those who take thought for the future of the city will need to take them into account equally with the emotional problems of history and the practical issues of administration.

This pamphlet might have been written in sombre terms as a record of the crimes men commit in the name of religion and under the stress of emotion. For Jerusalem is a real city, not a religious community of saints withdrawn from the world's life, and it bears constant witness to man's imperfections. It might tell of Christian massacres of Jews and Muslims, of hatred between brethren of the same religion, of Muslim cruelty and avarice, of Jewish terrorism, and of lying propaganda by men in high places, and still all would be true. But it would provide no foundation on which men could build wisely its future status. In relation to all three communities this side of the record has, therefore, as far as possible, been omitted; and it has been brought in only when it was essential to the understanding of the past and the planning of the future.

The fact that no party can get all it wants can be a basis for constant intrigue and bickering. But it need not be that. It can also be the basis for understanding and mutual co-operation. Because the word Jerusalem has meant so much in the world's history this is certainly what all men of good will should try to make it.

JAMES PARKES

Barley,
June, 1949.

The Story of
JERUSALEM

THE BIBLICAL STORY

ON THE eastern spur of a broad hill running southwards, protected
by a precipitous gorge on three sides but with higher mountains
lying around it, there stood three thousand years ago a tiny
fortified town of the Jebusites. It was called Urushalim, and its
castle bore the name of Zion. David, the warrior-poet king of
Israel, conquered it about 1000 B.C.E. and made it his capital.
On the site of an ancient place of sacrifice north of David's city,
Solomon, his son, raised a Temple to the God of Israel. The map
on the next page shows how the city grew and spread westwards
on to a broader, higher portion of the hill; but it cannot show
how it grew even more rapidly in the hearts of the people as a
symbol of the nation's life and religion. As ' Jerusalem ' or
' Zion ' it was the central symbol of the reign of righteousness to
which the incomparable succession of prophets called the Jewish
people—it is only necessary to look at a Biblical Concordance to
see how frequently the word was on their lips—and as prophetic
Judaism reached deeper into the understanding of true
Monotheism so also the name of Jerusalem grew to universal
significance as the place to which all peoples should turn ' for
out of Zion shall go forth the Law and the Word of the Lord
from Jerusalem.' While the prophets castigated its sins and its
political follies, they never wavered in their allegiance to its
religious significance.

This religious significance, in its turn, was never divorced
from the national destiny. The Temple of Solomon stood for less
than five hundred years, and perished with the kingdom of Judah
in 586 B.C.E. The people were taken captive to Babylon; and
from ' beside the waters of Babylon ' came the cry which echoes
all through Jewish history :

9

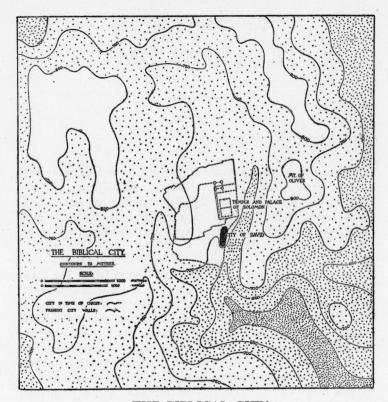

THE BIBLICAL CITY

They that led us captive required of us songs,
And they that wasted us required of us mirth,
Saying: Sing us one of the songs of Zion.
How shall we sing the Lord's song in a strange land?
If I forget thee, O Jerusalem, let my right hand forget her
   cunning.
Let my tongue cleave to the roof of my mouth if I remember
   thee not;
If I prefer not Jerusalem above my chief joy.

The exiles returned; the walls of the city, then the Temple, were rebuilt; national life was slowly restored. But for many centuries Jerusalem only changed one master for another, until it won a brief independence under the Maccabees. Then came Rome. The Temple was rebuilt by Herod the Great. But after two disastrous wars from A.D. 68—70 and 132—135, Jerusalem and the Temple were utterly destroyed and the Jewish people scattered through the world. But suffering and exile were ever linked with the hope of national revival in Jerusalem by the annual Passover service, which commemorated the early deliverance of the Israelites from the bondage of Egypt. At some early date—it is not known when—it became customary to end the service with the dramatic words : Next Year in Jerusalem.

THE LATER JEWISH STORY

WHEN THE Romans destroyed Jerusalem they built a heathen city on the site, and no Jew was allowed to enter it. But they soon crept back and settled on the western spur overlooking the ruined Temple. Gradually they came to be allowed to enter the city once a year to weep over its stones. Since then the Wailing Wall has been the central Jewish Holy Place in Jerusalem.

In the fifth century they were allowed to return, and soon became a substantial proportion of the population. After the Arab conquest in the seventh century they formed a whole quarter in the north-east part of the city. But when the Christian crusaders captured it in 1099 the Jews were gathered into the synagogue and massacred, and again no Jew was allowed to enter it. But twenty years later they returned once more; and since then Jewish life in Jerusalem has continued without a break, though they moved from the north-east to the southern quarter of the city, nearest to the Wailing Wall.

Misgovernment and the hostility of the population made life increasingly miserable. The city had no agricultural hinterland as did the cities of Galilee, and the Jews of Jerusalem were few compared with those of the latter cities right up to the nineteenth century. Sometimes only a few families were to be found there, sometimes they rose to a few hundreds. But they were rarely to be counted in thousands.

Few though they were the Jews of Jerusalem were regarded

by Jews throughout the world as their representatives in Zion, and they themselves felt the responsibility of this representative capacity. Their lives were spent in prayer and study; and it was actually among these Jews that there arose the only Jewish parallel to Christian monks, the Mourners in Zion, who pledged themselves to a life of poverty and prayer for the deliverance of their people. As the opportunities for earning even a meagre living dwindled through the increasing poverty and disorder of the whole land, it became the custom of synagogues everywhere to collect for the support of their brethren in Jerusalem. This kept alive the relationship when no alternative was possible, but much of the effort of Jewish philanthropists of the 19th century was devoted to works to secure for these Jews education, economic independence and medical care, and so to pave the way for the restoration of Jewish life in Palestine.

THE CHRISTIAN STORY

FOR THE Christian the name Jerusalem is inextricably associated with the life of the Founder of Christianity. Jesus of Nazareth was born in nearby Bethlehem, and though his early life and ministry were passed in Galilee, yet as a boy he visited Jerusalem and he taught beneath the colonnades of the Temple. And it was in Jerusalem that he was condemned by the priests and executed by the Romans.

For nearly three centuries the early Christians took little interest in the city. The apocalyptic vision of a new or heavenly Jerusalem which closes the New Testament served to replace the historic city in Christian minds, and there never developed any nostalgia for it such as was experienced by the Jews. It was not thought unfitting that its bishop should be subordinate to the archbishop of Cæsarea, and it was only in A.D. 451 that the Patriarchate of Jerusalem was established.

In the fourth century, having made his peace with the Church and himself accepted Christianity as his religion, the Roman Emperor Constantine began to build a new Christian city centering in two churches over the sites at which he believed the crucifixion and resurrection of Jesus to have taken place.

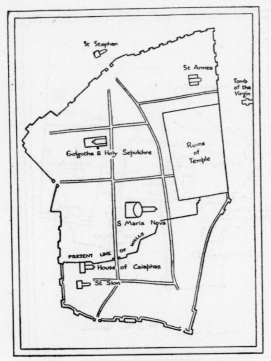

St Stephen

St Annes

Tomb
of the
Virgin

Golgotha & Holy Sepulchre

Ruins
of
Temple

S Maria Nova

PRESENT LINE OF WALLS

House of Caiaphas

St Sion

CHRISTIAN-ROMAN JERUSALEM

Jerusalem became a centre of Christian pilgrimage. This it has been ever since; and in every subsequent century thousands of Christians from all parts of the world have made the long and dangerous pilgrimage to the Holy City and the other shrines of the Holy Land.

A second Christian city was built between 1099 and 1187, when the Crusaders ruled Jerusalem. But, apart from this brief period, Christians have been satisfied if they could maintain their Holy Places undisturbed, and if pilgrims were allowed to visit them. The primacy was divided between the Greek Orthodox Patriarch and the Roman Catholic Guardian of the Holy Land, who was always a member of the Franciscan Order to which the care of their shrines had been entrusted by the Popes. But almost

13

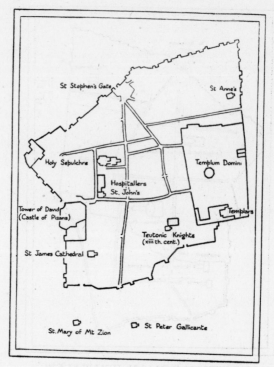

JERUSALEM OF THE CRUSADERS

all the ancient Christian Churches had their altars in the Church of the Holy Sepulchre and in other shrines, and most of them maintained convents in Jerusalem. At Easter century after century Christians from all parts of the world met as pilgrims in the Holy City, moved by a common devotion to their Master.

The holy places are described on p. 34 and are shown on the map on p. 35.

THE MUSLIM STORY

IT WAS after the death of Muhammad that Jerusalem was conquered from the Byzantines by his successor Abu-Bekr. In the

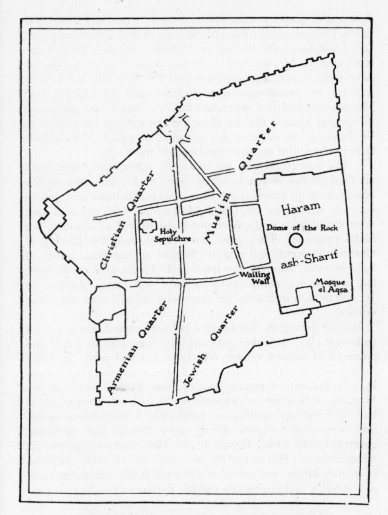

JERUSALEM OF THE MUSLIM RULERS

early days of his ministry Muhammad considered it the most sacred city on earth, and directed that Muslims should turn towards it in prayer. When he conquered Mecca he changed the

15

direction of prayer to that city, and made it the central shrine of Islam. His own association with Medina gave it the second place; and Jerusalem, with its two great shrines of the Dome of the Rock and the Mosque of Aqsa in the 'Noble Sanctuary' (Haram ash-Sharif), was finally acknowledged the third city of Islam. It was for its associations with Judaism and Christianity that Muhammad had first venerated the city, and it was the site of the Jewish Temple that he chose for the scene of his ' ascent to the heavens '. It was over this spot that the caliph Abd al-Malik built the beautiful shrine of the Dome of the Rock.

The association with the two older religions was recognised all through the eleven hundred years of Muslim rule. As the adjoining map shows, there were always Christian and Jewish quarters within the city; and Muhammad had enjoined that members of both faiths were not to be treated as idolaters, but to be protected. They paid heavy taxes, and the fleecing of Christian convents and pilgrims formed an important source of local revenue; many of the lesser Holy Places were confiscated; but even so for many centuries there was more toleration in Jerusalem than in Europe for those who differed from the ruling religion.

Muslim Jerusalem was never a political capital, but rather ' a cathedral city ', enjoying constant gifts from Muslim rulers and possessed of modest centres of scholarship and piety. Its great shrines were venerated throughout Islam, and it was often visited by pilgrims on 'the return journey from Mecca. Suleiman the Magnificent built its present walls in the sixteenth century, but it had little military significance. Unhappily it was allowed to fall into ever more complete decay under corrupt and inefficient governors until Abdul Hamid in the 19th century improved its administration. This paved the way for a considerable extension of its population, and added security led to the establishment of new suburbs and institutions outside the ancient walls.

JERUSALEM IN 1914

IT WAS the conquest of Palestine in 1831 by Mehmet Ali, Pasha of Egypt, which reopened the country to foreign visitors,

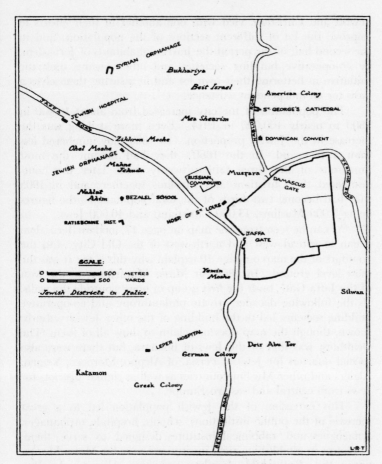

JERUSALEM IN 1914

and the moment coincided with a new interest of the western Churches, non-Roman as well as Roman, in Jerusalem and the ancient Churches of the East, and a new interest of western emancipated Jews in the lot of their oppressed brethren in the Holy City. Between 1840 and 1914 religious Orders, missionary societies, wealthy individuals and philanthropic organisations,

Jewish and Christian, vied with one another in their efforts to improve the lot of different sections of the population; and in the second half of the period the Jewish inhabitants of Jerusalem, by co-operative building societies and other means, took the initiative in bettering their own lot and in assuring themselves a basis for an independent existence.

The population of the city increased from about 10,000 in 1800 to nearly 100,000 in 1914. Even more striking was the increase in the Jewish proportion. In 1800 they numbered less than a thousand. In the 1860's they had become the most numerous of the three faiths; twenty years later they out-numbered the Christians and Muslims together; and in 1905 they had become two-thirds of the total population—the figures being 7,000 Muslims, 13,000 Christians, and 40,000 Jews.

As can be seen from the map on page 17, modern Jerusalem began to spread west and north-west of the Old City; and the contours of the map on page 10 explain why this is so : it was the most level ground. In 1860 Sir Moses Montefiore, to the west of the Jaffa Gate, built the first group of houses outside the walls. In the following decades private philanthropy and co-operative building societies led to the building of the other Jewish suburbs shown, though the map does not claim to show all of them. The wealthiest was that of the Jews of Bokhara, but there were also special quarters for Jews of Persia, of Aleppo, Morocco, Yemen, Algiers and other Muslim countries as well as similar districts for Jews from central and eastern Europe.

This extension of the Jewish population led to a great increase of the public institutions, schools, hospitals, orphanages, synagogues and rabbinical institutes designed to serve them. Foremost in establishing such institutions were Sir Moses Montefiore, the Rothschild family, and the Alliance Israélite Universelle. The increased numbers of the population made possible a considerable increase of economic activity, and improved security and the construction of first a carriage road, then a railway, joining Jerusalem with the coast, allowed of the development of a certain amount of trade with the outside world. Most of the skilled artisans in all branches of work had, from earlier times, been oriental Jews. These activities were still further stimulated by the coming of skilled Jewish workers from the West; and the whole development of this side of life was facilitated in 1906 by the erection, by German Jewish philanthropists, of the Bezalel School of Arts and Crafts. At the same time the Anglo-Palestine Company, founded by the World Zionist Organisation, brought the first example of modern banking into the country.

Although there was no similar extension of the Christian or Muslim population, the building of new Jewish houses outside the walls stimulated the wealthier Christians and Muslims to forsake the restricted quarters of the Old City. North of the Damascus Gate and in the south-west new Christian and Muslim suburbs arose. The main sign of Christian interest was, however, expressed in new institutions rather than in an increase of the number of Christians seeking residence in the city. Two suburbs were, nevertheless, built by western Christians, the German Colony by a group of German pietists known as ' The Temple', and the smaller American Colony by an American evangelist.

Of institutions there was a bewildering number, founded by different Roman Catholic Orders and by many non-Roman Churches. Most were entirely religious or philanthropic, although political prestige entered into the erection of some of the more prominent. Chief among these latter was the Russian Compound, built in 1860 and the following years, on the Maidan, the old assembly and parade ground of the city. Here arose a Russian cathedral and a vast enclosure of buildings intended to house and serve the thousands of Russian pilgrims who came annually to the Easter celebrations at Jerusalem.

The purposes of these institutions were various. Some devoted themselves to educational and medical work, some to work among the Jews, some to relations with the Eastern Churches, and yet others to Biblical research and archæology. The first to come was the London Society for the Propagation of the Gospel among the Jews, which established itself within the walls near the Jaffa Gate. Next, in 1841, an Anglo-Prussian bishopric was founded jointly by the Queen of England and the King of Prussia. After fifty years of existence it became exclusively Anglican, with a cathedral church of St. George on the Nablus Road and schools in Jerusalem and elsewhere. In 1847 the Latin patriarchate was re-established, and the Orthodox

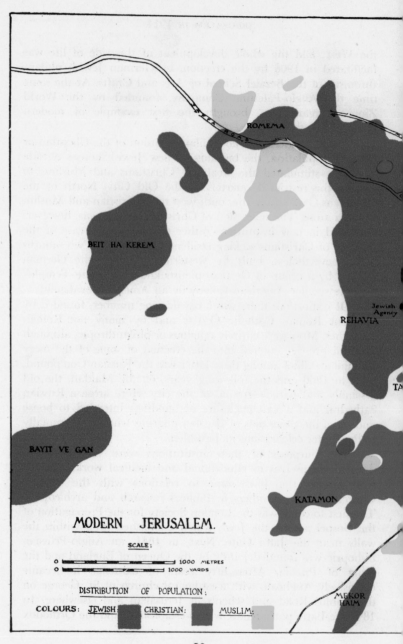

ROMEMA

BEIT HA KEREM

Jewish
Agency

REHAVIA

TA

BAYIT VE GAN

KATAMON

MODERN JERUSALEM.

SCALE:

0 ⊢━━━━━━━━━━━━━┥ 1000 METRES
0 ⊢━━━━━━━━━━━━━┥ 1000 YARDS

DISTRIBUTION OF POPULATION:

COLOURS: JEWISH: ⬛ CHRISTIAN: ⬛ MUSLIM: ⬛

MEKOR
HAIM

20

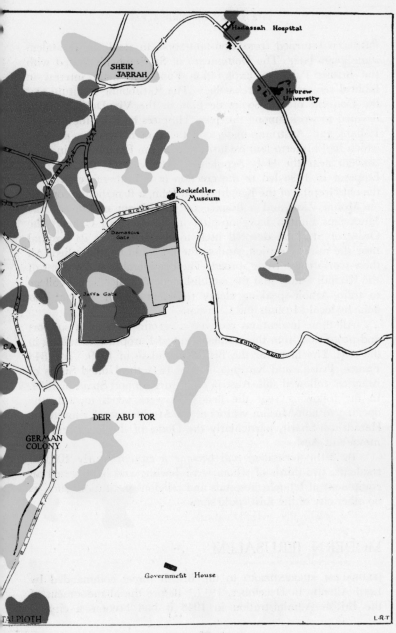

Hadassah Hospital

SHEIK JARRAH

Hebrew University

Rockefeller Museum

Damascus Gate

Jaffa Gate

DEIR ABU TOR

GERMAN COLONY

Government House

TALPIOTH

L·R·T

Patriarch returned from Constantinople to reside in Jerusalem some years later. The Dominicans of St. Stephen's shared with the British Palestine Exploration Fund the main interest in Biblical research and archæology. The Ratisbonne Institute and the Convent of the Sœurs de Sion in the Via Dolorosa were devoted to work among the Jews. Hospices built by the French, Italians and Austrians undertook the care of western pilgrims which had hitherto lain exclusively with the Franciscans in their convent near the Holy Sepulchre. The visit of the German Emperor in 1898 led to the erection of a Lutheran church on the old Hospital of the Knights of St. John, a Benedictine convent on Mount Zion and a hospice on the Mount of Olives. The Moravians built a leper hospital in the German Colony; the Order of St. John devoted itself to eye diseases in its hospital near the railway station. And so the list could be multiplied. All these works came from abroad. The considerable endowment of the Khalidi family and the establishment of a theological college to train Arabic-speaking clergy represent almost all that was done by local Muslims and Christians.

All these institutions received a certain amount of support and protection from the establishment of European consulates in the city. The first was the British consulate in 1839. In 1843 France, Prussia and Sardinia, and in 1844 the United States of America, followed suit. Austria came in 1849 and Spain in 1854. In the following year the first steps were taken towards the opening to non-Muslim visitors of the Muslim sacred sites in the Haram ash-Sharif, particularly the Dome of the Rock and the mosque of Aqsa.

By 1914 Jerusalem had become a city of nearly 100,000 residents, two-thirds of whom were Jewish; and it possessed an equipment of schools, hospitals and religious institutions such as no other city of the East could show.

MODERN JERUSALEM

JERUSALEM SURRENDERED to the British forces commanded by Lord Allenby in December, 1917. Before the abandonment of the British Administration in 1948 it had become a city of

160,000 inhabitants, of whom 100,000 were Jews and the rest were equally divided between Muslims and Christians. Of these two groups about 50,000 could be considered 'Arabs'. The overwhelming proportion of this population, of all faiths, lived in the new city outside the walls. Within them, still largely in the districts shown in the map on page 15, lived some 25,000 Muslims, Christians and Jews.

From the beginning of their Administration the British tried to preserve the historic character of Jerusalem by the protection and restoration of its monuments and by the careful control of its development. Considerable assistance was given to both Muslim and Christian bodies to enable them to repair mosques and churches, and to get their activities, upset by war conditions or previous Turkish misrule, into order. The ground round the walls was gradually cleared; building in the Old City was strictly controlled; and an open space was preserved round most of the walls and in the valley of the Kedron which framed the religious buildings of Mount Zion and the Mount of Olives. The familiar view of the walls and city was maintained unspoiled. Plans were constantly drawn and redrawn for the development and regulation of the new city, and though none of these plans were put integrally into effect, its general development compares favourably with that of any other city of its size.

At the beginning of the Mandate the city was without adequate water supply, electric light or drainage. There were few good roads except the main roads to Jaffa, Nablus and Hebron. These defects were gradually remedied. Water pumped up from the plain was accumulated in reservoirs on the high ground at Romema in the north-west. A sewage system was put into operation to drain both the old and new city, though it never caught up with the continual building of new suburbs. Old roads were improved and new roads planned, built and lighted to serve the ever-growing population; and many of them were planted with acacias, carobs and other trees. Open spaces were set aside and public gardens planted. Above all, building material was strictly controlled and the modern city rose in the beautiful gold and grey local limestone.

The Mandatory was slow to erect new administrative buildings, and its departments were housed in old hotels, hospices, ex-enemy buildings and the Russian Compound. But a new residence for the High Commissioner was built in a commanding position south of the city; a Government printing press rose in an impressive modern building near the railway station; and a new post office in the commercial district. A magnificent museum was built by John D. Rockefeller at the north-west corner of the walls. Jerusalem was throughout fortunate in its official architects.

The desire to serve all sections of the population animated many individual philanthropists who continued the tradition of the nineteenth century. An American built a vast Y.M.C.A., with hostel, lecture halls, gymnasium and athletic ground in which he hoped youth of all religions might meet. The Strauss Medical Centre in the city, and the new Hadassah Hospital on Mount Scopus, opened their doors to the sick of all communities; new schools, clinics, and institutes were opened and old ones extended.

In addition, each community erected buildings for its own use, and the city abounds in schools, churches, synagogues and institutions of all kinds. On the whole there has been least activity among the Muslims and the eastern Christians. To some extent their religious needs were met by the ancient churches, mosques and convents, while more modern institutions, such as schools, were provided for them by the Mandatory Power. But the Christians, at least, were handicapped by the poverty which resulted from the loss of many properties in Russia and elsewhere, and the Orthodox Church was crippled with debts.

Special mention must be made of the group of buildings forming the Hebrew University, the Jewish National Library and the Hadassah Hospital on Mount Scopus, not only because of their intrinsic importance to the whole Jewish community, but because of their isolated position north-east of the city. They constitute the academic and intellectual centre of the Jewish population of the whole country, and have already established their scientific value to the Middle East by their special studies and their agricultural, medical and scientific research and services. Before the war there were over a thousand students attending the different faculties, and in the quieter periods of the Mandate some of these were always Arabs; for though the formal teaching is in Hebrew, the University is open to all.

Jerusalem has become not merely a cultural and religious centre; it has a busy professional, commercial and industrial life. The law courts, the number and variety of its hospitals, the offices of the Palestine Potash Company, the Anglo-Palestine Bank and many other institutions have drawn to it an extensive professional class. Heavy industry was not permitted to establish itself by the Mandatory, but a wide variety of light industries was encouraged, including a revival of the traditional trades of pottery, glass-work and jewelry. In the district nearest the walls, and between the Damascus and Jaffa Gates, are modern shopping streets, the Arab shops being mostly nearest the two Gates, the Jewish in the wide area between them, in and around Ben Yehuda Street, King George's Avenue, Princess Mary Avenue and the Jaffa Road. There are a number of modern hotels, the largest being the ill-fated King David.

The map on pages 20 and 21 will show that the residential sections have, on the whole, continued to grow as relatively separate and homogeneous areas. The largest and most densely populated of these is the Jewish area which stretches to a width of nearly a mile on each side of the Jaffa Road as far as Romema. The most recent section of this area is the tree-embowered suburb of Rehavia, largely extended by refugees from Germany after 1933. The whole area is 90 per cent. Jewish, although it contains a number of Christian institutions, such as the new Abyssinian church, and the Ratisbonne Institute. It contains no 'Holy Places', though to the west of it there lies in a valley the ancient Monastery of the Cross, originally built by the Georgians in the sixth century.

West of this compact urban area is a chain of Jewish garden suburbs, Montefiore, Beth Hakerem and Bayit ve Gan. Beyond these is open country with a number of Arab villages, including Lifta, whose domination of the last stretch of the Jaffa Road into Jerusalem made it a hotbed of violence during the Arab riots of 1929 and the rebellion of 1936, and Deir Yassin, the scene of a massacre by Jewish terrorists in April 1948.

The character of the rest of the modern city is adequately shown by the map. While there are compact Christian, Muslim, and Jewish suburbs to the east and south of the Jewish area,

25

there is no single Christian or Muslim block, and the Jewish suburbs of Mekor Haim and Talpioth and the important group of the University and new Hadassah Hospital on Mount Scopus are completely detached from the Jewish area north-west of the city.

The formal division of the population into the three communities of Jews, Christians and Muslims conceals the cosmopolitanism and rich diversity of the city's life. Within each community was the widest variety, and, apart from modern politics, the divisions themselves concealed identities. There were as many Arabic-speaking eastern Jews as Arabic-speaking eastern Christians; many Muslims were not Arabs, and many Arabs were western-trained 'Europeans' in their culture and way of life. The old city within the walls was still a city of the East with its markets and intricate alleys, above all with the ancient Orthodoxies of its churches, synagogues and mosques. But its population covered scarcely one-sixth of the city's inhabitants; and the rest was primarily the creation of the West, partly of the Christian Churches, but above all of the Jewish population. These last have been the main source of its growth as well as the main centre of its cultural and professional life. Nor have they been the least hospitable and tolerant of the three communities. Their music and their medicine, their science and their scholarship, have provided an environment where, in time of peace, Jew, Christian and Muslim could meet and work together as citizens of one famous city.

GEOGRAPHICAL POSITION OF JERUSALEM

JERUSALEM STANDS over 2000 feet high on the eastern side of the Judæan hills, looking over the great cleft of the Dead Sea. On all sides it is only reached through mountainous country, and after the disappearance of the Roman roads it was only approachable on foot or horseback until the middle of the nineteenth century. Then a carriage way was made from Jaffa, which lies 35 miles away on the coast. At the end of the century a railway was also built joining Jerusalem to Jaffa and to the railway which passed up the coast, thence across the Jordan to

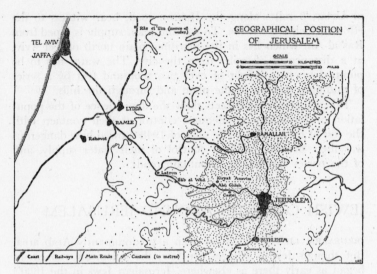

GEOGRAPHICAL POSITION OF JERUSALEM

join the line from Damascus to Medina through Transjordan. Roads joining Jerusalem to Nablus on the north, to Bethlehem and Hebron on the south, and to Jericho and Transjordan on the east were only made, or completed, by the British Mandatory.

Jerusalem is not surrounded by fertile country from which it can draw an adequate supply of vegetables and dairy produce. Its hills are stony, and made more so by centuries of soil erosion and neglect. In recent years both Arab and Jewish cultivators have remade miles of ancient terraces along the hills; but Jerusalem still needs to bring a large proportion of her food from the more fertile lands in the plains.

Even more serious is the lack of water supply. In the old city are many ancient cisterns for rain water, and several ancient pools. There is only one spring of any importance, that on the south-east side of the city (Rogel) which fills the pool of Siloam. But the supply of water from these sources is not only of uncertain quality and quantity but it is totally inadequate for the present population. Even in ancient days water was brought by aqueduct from a distance, and the three pools of Solomon

27

at Urtas, 8 miles along the Hebron road, bear witness to the efforts which were made. To-day the main supply is piped from Ras al-Ain which lies in the maritime plain north of Tel Aviv, at a distance of 35 miles from the city. The water has to be pumped up to a height of over two thousand feet by a series of pumping stations in the plain and through the hills.

Taken together these facts show the dependence of the population of Jerusalem on adequate control of their contacts with the rest of the country. The siege of 1948 showed how dangerous was their situation without control of their water supply, and of the passes through the mountain roads.

JEWISH COLONIES AROUND JERUSALEM

JERUSALEM LIES in what has been a predominantly Arab area. But though Jewish villages are few, the colonising movement began as early there as elsewhere. Jerusalem Jews in the 1880's founded Motsa on the road to Jaffa; and Har Tuv on the railway was begun in 1895. Both these villages are worked by individual farmers, as is Neve Ya'akob, founded on the road to Ramallah in 1924.

Most of the villages are, however, of the communal type which became the normal pattern in the Mandatory period. In them the settler has no private property but shares in the communal income. Children are cared for communally, but spend their evenings with their parents. There is no single and rigid form of these settlements, and they are constantly changing and developing, generally in the direction of greater individual freedom and family life. Some have been founded by Orthodox Jews; others are neutral in religious matters. While their main justification is their social significance as a new way of life, they are also much less costly to create than those where each farmer and his family must be separately established.

Of villages of this type Ataroth stands alone on the Ramallah road, and there are two groups of villages, one on the road to Jaffa and the other on that to Hebron. Kiryat Anavim was founded in 1922, and other villages were subsequently grouped around it. They stand across the valley from the Arab village

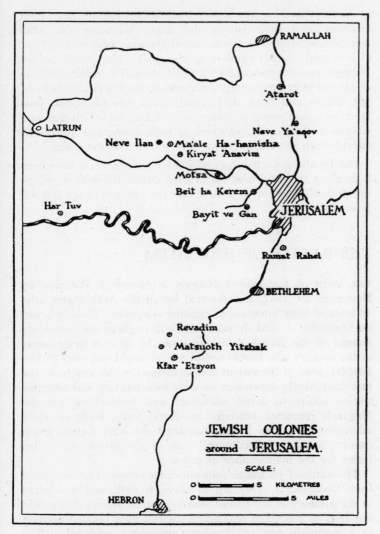

JEWISH COLONIES AROUND JERUSALEM

of Abu Ghosh with which they have always had the friendliest relations; and their woods and fields, balancing the Arab terraces and fruit trees, form one of the most beautiful sections of the road from Jerusalem to the plain. The group on the Hebron road has had a more tragic history. The original village of Migdal Eder was entirely destroyed during the Arab rebellion; but during and after the second world war Orthodox Jews founded a new group of villages on the land, of which the chief was Kfar Etzion. They stood on high, stony, and previously infertile hills with wide views over Judæa and the plain.

During and since the siege of Jerusalem settlements have been built along the new road, constructed during the siege to escape the Arab blockade, so as to overcome the isolation of the 100,000 Jews of the city.

THE BATTLE OF JERUSALEM

THE VOTE of the United Nations in favour of Partition on November 29, 1947, was rejected by all the Arab States, who announced their intention of resisting it by force. Rioting began on December 1, and disorder lasted throughout the remaining months of the British Administration. In spite of large forces in the country, the British would not, or could not, stop it. The 100,000 Jews of Jerusalem found themselves, almost from the first day, largely dependent on their own military and administrative ability to avoid starvation and destruction. Yet the Haganah remained officially an illegal force, while its chief adversary, the Arab Legion, attacked the Kfar Etzion group openly, although officially still part of the British controlled forces for the maintenance of order.

The battle of Jerusalem falls into three phases. The first lasted from December 1, 1947, up to May 14, 1948, and took place in the presence of the British Administration. During this period the Jews of Jerusalem realised to the full their isolated position in a mountain city all of whose approaches afforded endless opportunities for ambush and blockade. Within the city itself it was a period of bomb outrages by terrorists of both sides, of constant local battles in the mixed areas, of continuous sniping,

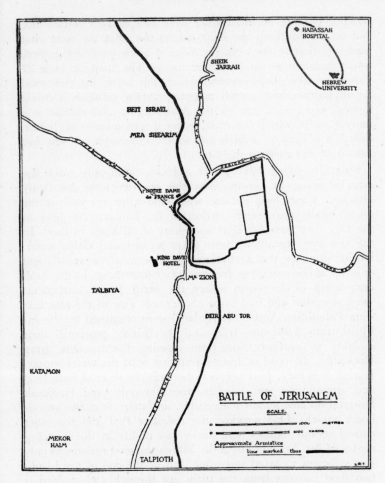

BATTLE OF JERUSALEM

and of the gradual evolution of specifically Jewish and Arab controlled districts. But the essential feature of this period was the battle for the roads.

The map on page 29 shows that there was no protection for the Jewish population of Jerusalem on the eastern road to

31

Jericho. On the northern road were two isolated settlements, and on the southern the Kfar Etzion bloc. But the most vital road was that to the west, for along it alone could come food, water, ammunition and reinforcements. The map on page 27 shows the key places around which the battle for this road raged. Latrun, with a vital pumping station, possesses a strong fortress which was held by the Arab Legion. Bal el-Wad is a narrow gorge where the road enters the mountains of Judæa. Castel is a ruin on a high hill which dominates all the last stretch of the road to the city.

From December 1947 Jewish vehicles could only reach the city by going in convoy, and the convoys were constantly attacked. Fresh food became short and after the end of the month mails were rarely delivered. By January the Jews of the Old City were besieged and short of all kinds of food. In the new city precautions were taken to save and ration water. During January the Arab forces became more organised, and enjoyed almost complete freedom of concentration in the Arab area north of Jerusalem where the small Jewish settlements were powerless and had to be abandoned. Few of the attackers were Palestinian Arabs. ' Irregulars ' were organised by the ex-Mufti from Syria and Iraq, and the British protested their inability to prevent them from crossing the frontiers, from blockading the road or from interfering with the water supply. During February, Jews began to be seriously short of both food and ammunition and supplies; the University and Hadassah Hospital became almost inaccessible, and there were two serious bomb attacks. One wrecked the *Palestine Post* and the other caused serious damage and heavy loss of life in the shopping centre of Ben Yehuda Street. By March the food ration was only just sufficient to avoid starvation, but at the end of the month two food convoys from the plain got through and enabled it to be maintained. At all costs the road had to be reopened.

Military supplies, in small quantities, had begun to trickle in, brought on men's backs along mountain paths, and hauled up cliffs by hastily improvised tackle; but by such means nothing could be done to feed the 100,000 civilians in the city. The city would fall if it proved impossible to break the blockade at Bal el-Wad and secure Castel so as to make a passage for lorries.

From April 3 to April 9 Castel was the scene of a violent struggle between the Haganah and the forces of the Mufti. The hill changed hands again and again, but finally the Arabs were driven out and the Jews obtained a secure possession of this vital spot. To get an equally secure hold on Bal el-Wad and Latrun proved impossible; but in the second half of April daring night attacks by wholly untrained troops succeeded in holding the road open long enough to get through two vital food convoys. Similar desperate means finally secured the whole mountain section of the road. But in the plain, and against the Arab forces in Latrun, such tactics by wholly untrained troops were valueless.

In the beginning of May a new phase opened. The Jews decided to construct an alternative road through uninhabited hilly country south of Latrun. So the 'Burma Road' came into being, and along its rough track more precious food convoys reached the city. Then a longer, but more secure and better graded, road was built which has been named the 'Road of Courage', but it was not in use until the siege was over.

Meanwhile in the city itself the Jewish population had improvised its defences. The northern settlements had fallen; it had proved impossible to secure the suburb of Sheik Jarrah and the Hospital and University remained isolated; the Jews in the Old City were still besieged; but in the new city they had strengthened their position in the southern suburbs by the seizure of Katamon. Almost the whole Arab population had fled long before. A heavy blow was suffered on May 14 when Kfar Etzion fell after a long and desperate resistance, and the task of defending the southern approaches fell to Ramat Rahel.

On May 15 the Arab Legion opened a new attack with artillery and armour from the north and east, while the Egyptians invaded Palestine from the south and, moving up through wholly Arab areas, approached Bethlehem. The Jews, however, had seized the 'security zones' evacuated by the British in the new city, and thereby consolidated their position. But in spite of the capture of Mount Zion they were unable to relieve the Jews of the Old City; it was reduced to a mass of rubble by artillery firing from the walls of the Haram ash-Sharif and surrendered on May 29. Though the road was cut again and the city totally invested, the Egyptians were prevented by the resistance of Ramat Rahel from joining up with the Arab Legion; and when this phase ended with the United Nations Truce of June 11, the Jewish hold on the new city was unbroken, and the Legion had done no more than capture Sheik Jarrah.

The Truce ended on July 9 and was reimposed on July 18. Although the food supply remained very low and the only piped water came from an emergency line opened by the Jews, and although continuous sniping and occasional shelling continued all through the summer and autumn, the new road prevented the isolation of the city, and it became evident that the Arab attack had been a military failure. But it was not until the end of November that fighting ceased. Not only had the city saved itself, largely by its own endeavours, but its resistance had destroyed the Arab plan of sweeping from east and south on to Tel Aviv, and so had saved the young State of Israel from destruction.

THE HOLY PLACES

THE REASON for the international concern with the future of Jerusalem is to be found in the presence of the 'Holy Places' shown on the adjoining map. Jerusalem is sacred to adherents of Judaism, Christianity and Islam.

The main Jewish Holy Place is the western wall of the great platform on which the Jewish Temple stood, known as the Wailing Wall. There are also an ancient cemetery and certain tombs. That these monuments are less conspicuous than those of the other religions is due to the fact that Jews expressed their devotion not so much by pilgrimage to special sites, but by the perpetual maintenance, through collections made throughout the Jewish world, of a Jewish population within the city. It was believed that their prayer and study would hasten the redemption of their people. The whole quarter in which these Jews lived, together with their ancient synagogues, was destroyed in the attack by the Arab Legion.

The Christian Holy Places are shown thickly scattered through the Old City and up the slopes of the Mount of Olives

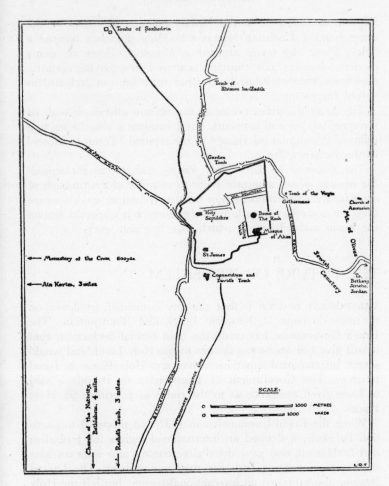

HOLY PLACES

to the east of it. It is, however, important to realise that there are almost equally important centres of Christian pilgrimage outside Jerusalem. The nearest of these are indicated by arrows; but Nazareth and the Sea of Galilee with Capernaum lie in the north of the Country, and the scene of the Temptation and the

35

Baptism of Christ lie in the Jordan valley to the east. On the other hand a Christian religious building does not become a 'Holy Place' by being situated in Palestine. There are many modern convents and churches scattered through the country, mostly on reputed Biblical sites; but these are not reckoned as 'Holy Places'.

The Muslim shrines centre in the Haram ash-Sharif with its mosques, schools and convents. But Jerusalem is also the starting point of the annual pilgrimage to the reputed 'Tomb of Moses' in the Jordan valley.

The dispersal of these Holy Places and shrines throughout the country is an important point to consider in the problem of their future administration. For both in Jerusalem and elsewhere they are not apart from human dwellings, but dispersed among the towns and villages in which men live and work.

THE FUTURE OF JERUSALEM

THE PRESENT position is that the city is divided, as shown on the map on page 31, between Israel and Transjordan. The Israeli Government has made the most formal declaration that it will give full access to pilgrims to the Holy Land, and would accept international supervision over any Holy Places in Israel territory. The Government of Transjordan on its side is said to have given assurance as to the rights of pilgrims and Holy Places.

When the Royal Commission in 1937 first proposed to partition Palestine, it devised an international regime for Jerusalem and Bethlehem, and gave the regime control of a wide corridor to the sea containing both the road and railway. The United Nations also proposed an international regime, but left the Holy City, including the population of 100,000 Jews, as an island in the Arab State. Count Bernadotte in his first proposals went even further and proposed that the whole city should be given to the Arab State; but just before his tragic assassination he had reverted to the idea of an international administration. To-day the most outspoken advocate of an international régime is the Vatican.

This pamphlet has dealt largely with the Jewish concern because the obvious problem which an international regime would have to face is the security and development of the Jewish population. It is neither practical nor moral to brush this on one side; and it would be difficult to find evidence in any of the three religions involved that God set more store by the holiest sites than by the lives of men, women and children. The Jewish argument against an international regime is simple. It is the evidence of the battle of Jerusalem, weighed against the facts that the regime would have no control of the roads, that the stability, efficiency and impartiality of the United Nations is impossible to assume, and that no one has suggested where the immense sum of money is to come from which such an administration and its garrison would require.

There are, however, two other questions of importance. The first is that the access of pilgrims to the Holy Places of Jerusalem and Bethlehem would in any case depend on the good will of the Jewish and Arab States; the second is that not all the Holy Places are in the Jerusalem area.

The argument has been used that the Jews should make the sacrifice of their feelings and surrender Jerusalem ' in response to the concern of millions of Christians for the Holy Places '. Even if we accept that (without propaganda) millions of Christians are both informed and agitated, I think we could only expect Jews to give precisely the answer which we should ourselves give in similar circumstances. Had the millions of Christians, the Churches, and the governments which use this argument, made a serious, even if unsuccessful, attempt to prevent the battle of Jerusalem or to relieve the Jewish civilians, women and children, when they were on the point of starvation, they would at least have a moral right to put it forward. As it is, they have not.

One argument, however, is advanced for an internationally controlled Jerusalem which has little to do with Holy Places; it is that it is impossible to divide the city. Nobody would disagree that the proposal to divide a city which has grown as a unity is both regrettable and difficult; that it will involve anomalies, inconveniences and loss; but it has to be considered, not *in vacuo,* but in relation to the alternatives which have been discussed

37

above; and it is difficult to argue that they offer an easier or more satisfactory solution. It happens that the way in which modern Jerusalem has been built, in separate community suburbs, probably makes it easier than in many cities; and there are long sections where a frontier could be made to pass through open spaces and unbuilt-up areas. In so far as the living inhabitants of the city are concerned, partition appears to be the least disadvantageous solution offered.

On the other hand there are strong arguments against an arrangement which left direct responsibility for the Holy Places in the hands of either a Jewish or an Arab government, even though these arguments have little to do with Jewish, Christian or Muslim conceptions of 'holiness'. The Holy Places in the past have been the scenes of such fanaticism and mutual intolerance and have been exploited for such political purposes that to entrust to either government the responsibility for order and the adjudication of claims concerned with religious bodies of faiths other than their own would be to entrust them with a difficult, distasteful and perhaps impossible task. It would not be easy for either Jew or Muslim to adjudicate between Roman Catholics and Greek Orthodox, over rights in the church of the Holy Sepulchre; for Jews to be responsible for the festival of Nebi Musa, or for Muslims to regulate the Wailing Wall. If the arguments for an international political sovereignty over Jerusalem or some part of it are weak, the argument for an international commission with a direct responsibility for all Holy Places situated within governments of a different faith is very strong.

In the present state of the United Nations it would certainly be more practical to suggest that they negotiate a treaty with both Israel and the Arab State, by which each Power, in addition to guaranteeing the maintenance of Holy Places, and the access to them under suitable conditions (e.g. unarmed and for a defined period) of pilgrims of the religion concerned, would pledge itself to allow an international commission under the United Nations rights of inspection, of the adjudication of disputes, of the certification of pilgrims, and of other necessary matters. Both powers have, in fact, behaved well apart from the inevitable excesses of war; both have stated their willingness to give the necessary guarantees for the immunity and protection of Holy

Places. There at least is a starting point from which something might be built. Nor is it cynical to add that it would probably work well because it is thoroughly in the interests of both powers, and to their economic advantage, to see that it did.

Perfect solutions rarely exist in an imperfect world. A political division of the city, and an international commission charged with the care of the Holy Places, offer the best chance of working, and therefore of creating relations between the two peoples which might lead to enduring peace.